15 Minute Finance

What School Didn't Teach You

Richard Chater

15 Minute Finance: What School Didn't Teach You by Richard Chater

Published by Richard Chater

www.richardchater.com

Cover by Richard Chater.

ISBN: 978-1-7397655-0-7 (print)

Printed in the United Kingdom

First Edition

Contents

INTRODUCTION

If you had a pound for every time you heard someone complain about not being taught about personal finance in school, you wouldn't need this book! So many people needlessly dread the thought of managing their finances; hopefully through the course of these pages, however far you get, that stress will diminish. The seemingly endless pit of unknown finance knowledge may start to shrink within reach – because it is! Whether you have 15 minutes, an hour or a day, there's something for you here.

I strongly believe that personal finance shouldn't be consumed by frugality! So many people see those two things as synonyms when they really don't need to be. In this book I promise to never tell you to change your lifestyle. This is going to be all about adapting the way that you buy the products and services that you're already using so that they cost less or get you cashback, then getting the most out of the money you have left over!

Over a number of years developing knowledge and opinions on personal finance, I've optimised my own finances and gotten to a point where I'm now satisfied with my long-term plan. However, this has left me in a sticky spot: I'm left with this knowledge and have a very limited ability to utilise it any further because everything is in place. There's only so long you can be pleased with yourself after you switched your current account to get cashback on your bills! After years of helping my friends to replicate all of the things I've been doing to save and make money, I have decided to increase my reach through the medium of this book, in which, I will summarise what I wish I knew when I started to arrange my finances.

It's about more than information though, isn't it? So many people have a rough idea of what they could be doing, but don't think they have the time or effort to sort it all out. Which brings us to my second goal: to show you all how quick and easy this can be. To prove that personal finance isn't a thing to be feared – whether you have 15 minutes, an hour, or a day, you can still take the reins on your financial life! I will start off by explaining what I think you can do in 15 minutes, then I will move on to explain the best things I think you could do in just an hour set aside for your finances and finally we will take a day to try and round everything off. The things in the first 15 minutes aren't necessarily the most impactful, but they're the best you can do with 15 minutes in my opinion, so to get the most out of this process make sure to read to the end!

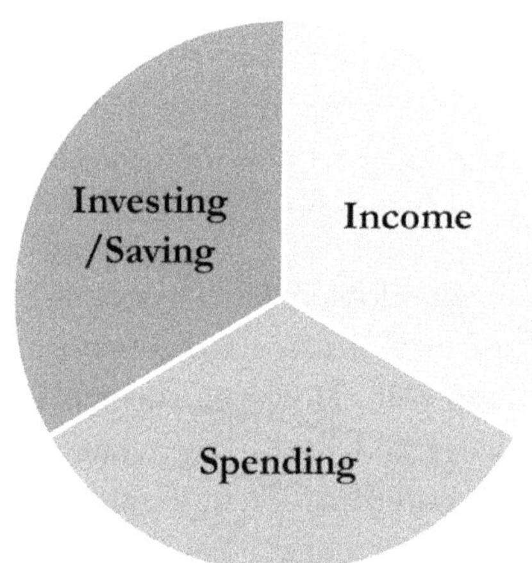

In my view, managing your finances can be filtered down into three main focuses as I have shown in the pie chart above. For the first 15 minutes we will be primarily focussing on income and spending. Approaching this through the benefits of switching current account as well as getting discounts and cashback on the spending you're already doing.

For the next hour we'll then focus mostly on laying the foundations of a strong credit score and finish off spending optimisation through bill comparison. There will also be a sprinkling of 'income' in there from the perspective of credit card cashback and introductory bonuses, rounding off the discussion of current accounts from the first '15 minutes'.

We will then end things with (in my opinion) the scariest of the great triad: Investing/Saving. We will go into savings, debt, retirement, your home as an investment and finally a brief overview of the stock market. I was very torn when deciding where to place this section in the book. I strongly believe that this section is likely to have the largest long-term impact on your finances by a significant margin. At the same time, I think it's important to appreciate that it also requires the greatest time commitment. With the potential for strong long-term gains, also comes the potential for strong long-term losses (or at least, imperfect gains). With this in mind, the '1 Day' section can also be read independently and will happily thrive as its own entity. I would still recommend the natural order, because if all goes well, the 15 minute and 1 hour sections will give you more money to save, invest or pay off debt!

With everything I discuss in this book, I absolutely recommend that you do your own reading on each topic before you make any decisions. This book is a summary of what I would do if I were to go back in time, and best used as a summary/index which should be used as a leap-pad to start your personal finance journey!

Finally, throughout the book I will give links and QR codes for the products or services that I mention. If available, I will use an affiliate link which typically means you and I will get a bonus if you go through my link. In the interest of being impartial, I will always let you know if a link will lead to me getting a bonus, as well as a set of generic links (that I don't get a bonus from) at the end of the book.

15 MINUTES

Introduction

For a lot of people, the simplest and easiest way to make strides with your finances is to clean up what is already there! There are all of the things I'm sure you've heard dozens of times before: Going through bank statements and cancelling unused subscriptions; paying off debt; transferring debt to 0% or low interest alternatives; asking your boss for a raise and reducing the takeaways you buy. Whilst these may be appropriate first steps, they definitely don't squeeze inside 15 minutes, and more importantly they go against the number 1 rule I set out earlier: to not force frugality on you! So, in this section I'm going to talk more about what you can do without changing the lifestyle you already have.

The way we're going to do that first is by giving you small universal savings. Ways of getting a small amount of cashback or discounts often, creating up to a few hundred pounds every year.

Current account

Right now, it's easier than ever to switch current accounts. Once upon a time it may have been a daunting endeavour, but thanks to the current account switch guarantee you can switch your current account seamlessly. When you go through the application form to open a new current account, if you want to switch, you can input your old account details and the bank will take care of the rest! They'll switch over your regular payments, your balance, redirect incoming payments and close your old account for you so there's nothing else you need to do! Admittedly, some benefits end after a certain period, for example incoming payments will typically only be redirected for 3 years automatically, so make sure you check all of your important payments and the terms if you switch.

I would broadly categorise current accounts into the four types shown in the diagram on the next page, but we're on a timer, so let's focus on **cashback** and **introductory bonuses**! I'll cover the other two types more later on.

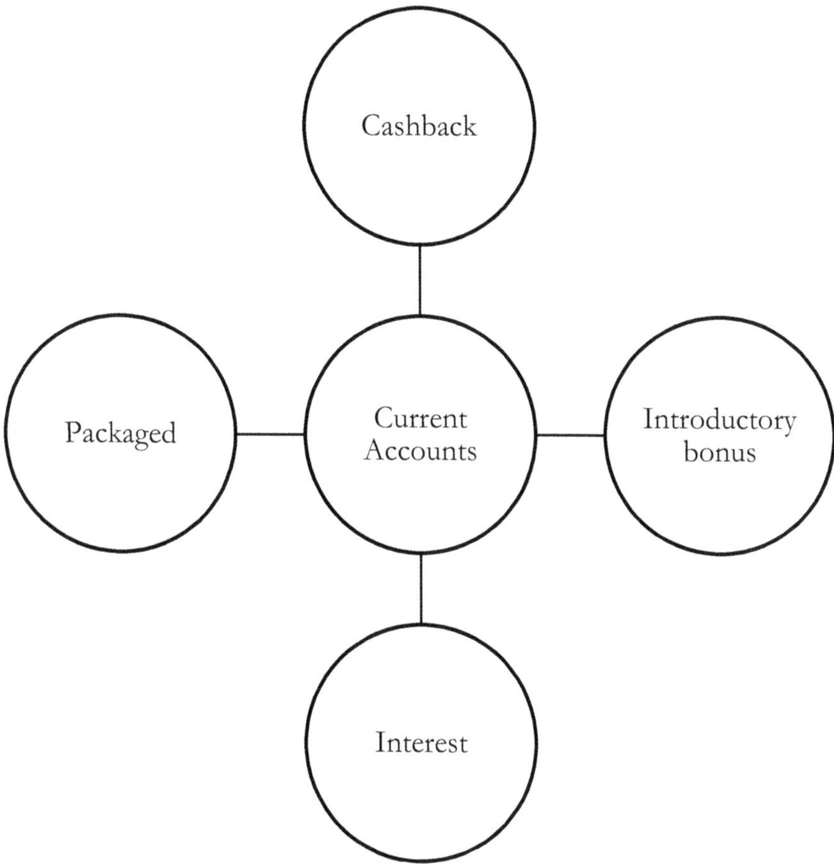

Cashback from current accounts come in two main forms: bill cashback and spending cashback. The first is typically better for the average person because you can usually get a higher cashback percentage and for most people bills make up a large amount of their monthly expenses. Debit card spending cashback is rarer and normally has a lower rate. Banks charge the vendor (e.g. shops and restaurants) every time you use your card, because of this, some generous banks give a small amount of that back to you (the best at the time of writing is about 1%). Because of the nature of this cashback, they're best compared to cashback credit cards and as such I'll go into a bit more detail about these later. For now, they're a great way of getting consistent cashback in a way that doesn't risk accumulating debt.

Introductory bonuses are the next point of focus! Your custom is really valuable to banks, they want you to have your main current account with them because they can invest your money and make a small percentage off every transaction you make. This means that sometimes, they're willing to go above and beyond to lure you in with big switch bonuses. Right now, you can expect to get over £100 as a bonus and occasionally you may find banks offering big ticket items like headphones or cases of wine!

They will probably have conditions you need to meet to get their bonus. They might want you to have a certain amount of money going into the account each month (typically around £1000), but they don't usually care where this comes from or how long it stays there. Therefore, if there is a pay-in threshold, you can set up a monthly standing order from a different bank (it can be yours or somebody else's) and then set up a second standing order back to the original account. That way you can recycle the same money again and again and as far as the bank is concerned, you're paying in the amount they want (always check with the bank if you're allowed to do this, it's never been a problem for me though). If this sounds a bit complicated, have a look at the diagram below. Once you've got your head around it, it's just two standing orders and you can sit back and relax! The obvious downside of this option is that you need the £1000 in your account to transfer around in the first place.

The other big condition that these bonuses often have is that you may need a certain number of direct debits going out every month, so make sure you have the right number to get the bonus! It is important to keep in mind that when you apply for a current account, they'll do a 'hard search' of your credit report. This can have a negative effect on your credit score and will stay on your report for up to 2 years, so if you're planning on getting debt e.g. a credit card or mortgage in the next 2 years, keep this in mind. I'll explore credit scores in a bit more detail in the next section.

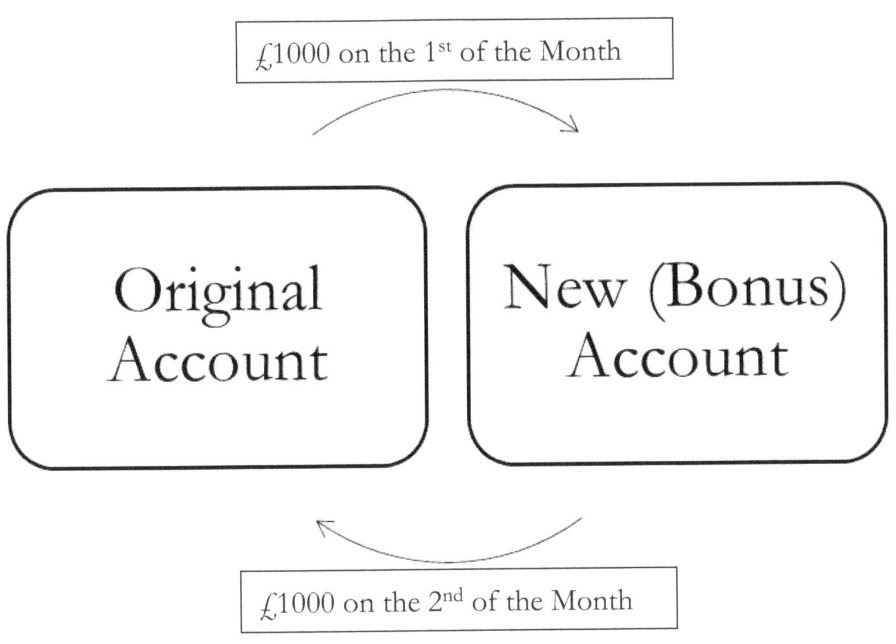

A really important thing to note when it comes to current accounts, that often gets overlooked is that you aren't limited to one current account. You're allowed to have as many current accounts as you desire, as long as you hit any requirements that each of them may have. Personally, I have 4 current accounts: One that my bills come out of, that gives me cashback on bills; one that I only use for debit card payments because I get cashback on debit card transactions; a packaged account through which I get very cheap breakdown cover, phone insurance and travel insurance; and finally, a joint account with my partner.

To compare what you can get from different banks, my favourite place is MoneySavingExpert – the home of the *Emperor of Personal Finance:* Martin Lewis. Here's a QR code and a link:

www.moneysavingexpert.com/banking/compare-best-bank-accounts

Cashback chrome extensions

Second up comes chrome extension cashback/ discounts. They won't make you rich, but only take a couple of minutes to set up, and then you can pretty much forget about it and they can accumulate to over £100 a year! Although that may sound complicated it's quite simple when you break it down. If you use google chrome, you can add on these applications which track which websites you're on and they'll ping when you can save money!

Honey is my favourite because it's so simple! It is a chrome extension which has a catalogue of discount codes for loads of popular (and unpopular) shops online. When you get to the checkout, you can click the honey logo in the top right corner of your screen (have a look at the screenshot below) and it will try out all the voucher codes it has saved! One button click and you'll be left with a tasty discount!

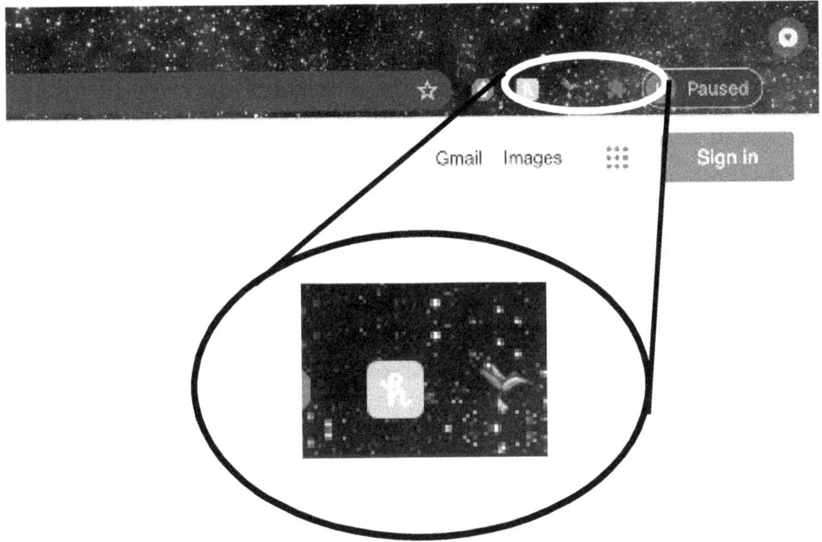

The second and final chrome extension that I will mention is **TopCashback** (seen to the right of honey in the screenshot). This one may take 5 minutes to set up, because you have to make an account so it's a bit more long winded but still well worth it! They, as the name implies, offer cashback. The chrome add-on will ping when you're on one of their partner websites to let you know you can get cashback. Then you can click the link and wait a few seconds while TopCashback does its thing before redirecting you back to the website you were on. A few important things to note here are when you start out, you have to make an account with them; you need to specifically request your cashback to be paid out, otherwise it will sit in a holding account on the website (they do send reminder emails about this if you forget though) and finally you usually need to click the extension in the top right of your browser when you start shopping. That means if you forget about it until you're at the checkout, you may need to go back and add everything back to your basket again – a bit of a faff, but in my opinion well worth it.

www.joinhoney.com/ref/jm7cfc4

Affiliate Link

www.topcashback.co.uk/ref/richardchater

Affiliate Link

Special Discounts

Finally, a quick mention to specialised discount services like Blue Light Card for NHS, emergency services or armed forces employees and Unidays (or many more alternatives) for students. They're full of amazing discounts for a huge variety of shops, eateries and services. If you're eligible for one of these, signing up can be one of the best uses of personal finance time out there! The main downside here is that you have to go searching for the discounts on their website – no handy add on this time.

www.bluelightcard.co.uk

www.myunidays.com

1 HOUR

Introduction

Now we can really get into it! 15 minutes isn't a very long time, so now it's time to build a financial palace on top of those foundations we've built! We're going to talk about the importance of a credit score and how to build it, along with the value and risks of credit cards with a bit of healthy myth dispersion! Finally, we'll round off our hour by looking at reducing our costs again, this time through the lens of bills!

In this section we start to talk about credit (debt), which inherently carries risk, so remember to keep doing your own research in parallel to this book. Remember that this isn't financial advice, just a snapshot of what I know and my opinions!

I won't go into detail about what to do if you find yourself in trouble with debt. If you feel stressed about your debt or you feel that it is having a significant impact on your life, there are a number of places you can look for help and advice. Three good examples of places to go are: National Debtline, a charity which give free debt advice from trained professionals; Citizens Advice, another independent charity who can give advice through web chat or over the phone; and finally if you would prefer a 'self help' style option, Money Saving Expert have a great article on debt problems. If you want to check out any of these options, follow the links on the next page!

nationaldebtline.org

www.citizensadvice.org.uk

www.moneysavingexpert.com/loans/debt-help-plan

Credit Score

I was incredibly close to putting this in the 15-minute section, I think it's incredibly important to set things in motion early for your credit score and develop an understanding of what will affect your credit score. You need your credit score to start credit agreements, this includes credit cards, current accounts, car finance and most importantly (in my opinion) a mortgage. At the start, my view of debt was 100% on credit score – I made sure at every stage that I didn't view my credit as my money, my credit card was a way of increasing my credit score, never to be viewed as a way of being able to afford more. When thinking about my credit card:

- If I couldn't comfortably pay it off at the end of the month, I wouldn't pay with a credit card
- If I wouldn't buy it with a debit card, I wouldn't buy it with a credit card

I started optimising my credit score when I was 17, I got to the maximum Experian credit score of 999 by 21 and bought my first property when I was 22. Importantly though, it's never too late to start and it's not as hard as you think! In the UK we don't have a nationalised credit score, that means broadly speaking, banks/ financial institutions make their decision on your trustworthiness in their own way. This means when you get a credit score from places like Experian or ClearScore, they should only be used as a guide. As you may know, when you use credit score services, they won't tell you if you are eligible for a product of not, they will only be able to tell you if you're likely or unlikely to be eligible. In extension to this, everything I say here should be taken with a pinch of salt, credit score isn't calculated in the same way everywhere and banks will use more characteristics than I mention and won't use some of the things I mention at all.

The most important thing that will affect your score long term is how you have handled credit (debt) in the past. Broadly, this includes:

- Repaying on time
- How much credit you have and how much of it you use on a monthly basis
- How long your credit relationships have lasted in the past
- Lots of other factors

So, what can a person do to control these things? When it comes to repaying on time, you can usually automate this, so it's not on your shoulders to remember to pay. You should always repay credit cards in full at the end of the month, this way you won't end up paying interest but you still get all of the benefits which I'll talk about more later in this section. You can guarantee that this will happen by arranging payment in full by monthly direct debit which, you may remember, this has the added benefit of helping you hit the eligibility requirements for certain current accounts!

With regard to the amount of credit you have, the magic phrase is **'utilisation ratio'**. This, put simply, is how much of your credit limits you use (primarily credit cards). Different sources give different answers but typically between 10% and 50% of your monthly limit is recommended. Lenders want to see that you're using your cards and not forgetting about them but more importantly, that you're 'responsible' and not maxing them out. Some recommend that you put one recurring thing on your credit card e.g. your groceries, weekly takeaway or some subscriptions. Finally, you can adjust your credit limit so that it fits inside the 10% to 50% range.

Let's go through some example numbers! *Please do your own research, these numbers are for demonstration only.* If I spend £200 a month on groceries, I set my credit limit to £1000 so that my 'utilisation ratio' is 20%. If I was starting out and I could only get a £200 credit limit, I may put my daily £3 meal deal on the credit card, that way I've got £60 a month on the card giving me a utilisation rate of 30%. By doing this, you will use some credit every month and it should never be a large burden to pay off at the end of the month, and most importantly it is something you would be paying for anyway. Overall (with a bit of luck) after all of this, banks will see you as a more responsible and reliable person to lend to when it comes time to get a mortgage!

Finally, there are a bunch of other things that can contribute to credit score that don't involve debt:

- Being on the electoral register
- Having up to date details with your utilities and banks e.g. name and address
- Duration of financial relationships i.e. how long have you had your oldest current account?
- Credit searches
    - This is when a company looks into your history/ credit report, to work out if they want to do business with you. It happens whenever you apply for credit or a current account among other things. You should always be told when an organisation is going to do one. They can last up to 2 years on your credit report, so if you're planning on applying for a credit card/mortgage etc soon, bear this in mind

Now I've spoken about one of the main benefits of credit cards, let's talk about the rest of the pros and cons. Here is a tasty table to get a flavour of credit cards at a glance:

Credit Cards	Debit Cards (Without Overdraft)
Larger purchases are insured	No extra insurance
Cashback on purchases more common	Less options if you want cashback on purchases
Will cost more if you don't pay in full every month	No interest paid on purchases
Debt	Not debt
Build credit score	Doesn't affect credit score

Before we go any further, it's important to discuss risk stratification. It can be very hard to conceptualise and balance the risk of debt and because of this I think this is the most commonly misconceived aspects of a credit card. Lots of people are wrongly terrified of debt and lots of people are wrongly nonchalant about it. Debt can be an incredibly powerful tool, especially when buying a home or starting a business. However, importantly both of these have tangible financial benefits, so by using debt you are increasing your long term financial potential. Using debt i.e. a credit card to purchase luxury items such as clothes or cars creates a very different dynamic. Not only do they decrease your long term wealth, but credit cards have very high interest rates, meaning that the effect of these purchases can compound aggressively leading to much more substantial effects on your finances. Because of their very high interest rates, credit cards are often described as 'bad debt'. If you only pay the 'minimum payment' on your credit card, you will often end up paying off your purchases many times over. To put that in perspective, if you had a balance of £5000 on a credit card at 20% APR interest, you could pay off £1000 a year until the end of time and you would still owe £5000.

The future doesn't have to be bleak if you're in a position like this though! There are balance transfer credit cards, which I won't go into much detail on, but I feel that they deserve to be briefly mentioned. These are cards which allow you to transfer debt from another card without interest for a certain period, usually 1 or 2 years. In situations like the example above, it's easy to feel like you're drowning, with the significant cost of interest, it can be hard to pay down the principle. It's as if you're in a boat that is letting in water, but your bucket is only big enough to bail out water as fast as its coming in, leaving you ankle deep in water indefinitely. Balance transfer cards can give you 24 months without any metaphorical water coming into your boat, giving you time to bail out the water that's already up to your ankles!

Now let's explore three of those important differences in more detail: **cost**, **insurance**, and **cashback**. First, **cost**. The aim of the journey we've embarked on in this book is to strengthen our financial positions. If we start paying interest on all of our purchases, our costs will go through the roof, and we could end up in a real pickle! As I just mentioned, credit card debt is typically quite bad debt, it has a high interest rate and its quite easy to unexpectedly build up because you don't have to sign a contract each and every time you use your card! The solution? Pay your credit card off in full every month! This way you get the benefits of a credit card like credit score, cashback and insurance without having to pay any interest.

Secondly, credit cards have **insurance** built in for purchases of products or services that cost between £100 and £30 000. This means that the credit card company has equal liability for that product as the seller if there is a fault or problem with the purchase. This gives an advantage to credit cards versus debit cards when making larger purchases. For example, if you bought a holiday on your credit card and the holiday company went bust, you would still be eligible for a full refund from your credit card company in most circumstances thanks to section 75 of the Consumer Credit Act!

We spoke about **cashback** briefly before when discussing debit cards, now how about credit cards? Credit cards typically charge merchants more on each purchase than a debit card. This means credit card companies can afford to give a bit more of that back to you, the card holder, compared to debit cards. The best example of this is American Express who charge merchants more in processing fees (somewhere around 2-3%) and because of this are able to offer you higher cashback of around 1-1.5% typically. The other side to this is that you could be harming small businesses with high merchant fees if you use one of these cards. I personally reconcile the morality of this by using my debit card more often when I'm at small independent businesses like my local takeaway and using my credit card when I'm shopping with large businesses.

Finally, **how do you decide on a credit card?** I focus on two main factors when making this decision, what are the benefits? And how likely am I to be approved for the card? My favourite tool to research this is, once again, the Money Saving Expert comparison tool. Using a comparison site before you apply should reduce the likelihood of being refused, because the comparison tool will give you an idea of how likely you are to be accepted before you apply using a 'soft search'. A soft search means they take a surface level glance at your credit history in a way that won't affect your credit score. This is important because when you actually apply for a credit card, they will perform a 'hard search' which will affect your credit score. This means that if you're rejected, if you try to apply for a different credit card straight away, you're less likely to be accepted. I like Money Saving Expert because they're relatively impartial compared to some other comparison sites, but it's worthwhile trying out a few different comparison tools anyway because different sites have different sponsorships/endorsements, so you may get a better deal elsewhere.

www.moneysavingexpert.com/eligibility/credit-cards/search

Comparison websites

Moving smoothly on from credit card comparison to bill comparison! Energy bills and insurance are the biggies here, while a lot of people are used to shopping around for insurance, anecdotally I think it's less common for people to consider comparison for energy. The same overarching principles follow through from credit card comparison: most comparison sites have biases, so try a couple to make sure you're getting the best deal. Taking the first step is the most important thing, using a comparison site should lead to a good saving, then every time you use a different site, it will make a smaller and smaller difference each time. If you're struggling to fit this into the prescribed 1 hour of financial education, 1 comparison site is a lot better than 0 sites.

When it comes to **energy** comparison, you may have guessed, my favourite tool is with Money Saving Expert! This one comes with an especially strong recommendation: it's my favourite Money Saving Expert tool, because it comes with the option to sign up to email notifications to let you know if a better deal has become available for you, and as with all Money Saving Expert tools, its completely free! Truly the stuff dreams are made of…

You will be faced with the option of fixed rate vs variable rate tariffs, the difference here is that a fixed rate locks you in at the same price for a year, which means if the price of energy goes up (which it typically does) the price of your bills will stay the same for the year. The flip side of this is that if the price of energy goes down, you'll typically have to pay an early exit fee to drop down to that cheaper tariff if you want it. A really nice combination that occasionally appear are fixed tariffs with £0 exit fees, this means you have the ability to lock in a cheap tariff with the peace of mind that you can swap to another provider or tariff if prices go down!

The other big factor to look out for is single rate vs two rate tariffs. A two-rate tariff has a lower cost of energy during the night and a higher rate during the day. These tariffs may be cheaper for people that that use a lot of energy during the night e.g., people that charge electric cars and people that have storage heaters. As a rule of thumb this isn't normally something you are expected to choose. Normally when you move into a property, it will already have the right type of meter installed and you can stick with whatever is already there. It's definitely worth discussing with your provider if you think you're not getting the best option though!

Finally, you can consider whether they will offer you a smart meter (which is estimated to save you around 2% according to Smart Energy GB). Smart meters are small screens which give you a live reading of your energy consumption to help you to get a better understanding of how you use energy. Truly my final comment on energy: you can also consider whether your energy provider uses 'green' energy such as wind or solar. As a nice coincidence, the cheapest energy providers also typically use green energy, but it's still worthwhile double checking when you're picking your provider.

www.clubs.moneysavingexpert.com/cheapenergyclub

Insurance comparison is typically a lot simpler, there are less variables that you can control. The biggest determinants of your costs are mostly out of your hands, such as postcode, occupation and the make and model of your car. Nonetheless, you can consider a few things: you can tweak your job title (within the confines of the truth) e.g. teacher vs primary teacher, student vs mature student, accountant vs chartered accountant. Counterintuitively, when searching for car insurance, parking your car on your drive is often cheaper than parking in a garage. And finally, the most well-known trick: named drivers. With this last one, whilst it can save a lot of money on car insurance, you need to make sure that the named driver is truly going to be driving the car, otherwise it may be classed as fraud and invalidate your insurance. Always check in advance and if in doubt, call up your insurance provider.

www.comparethemarket.com

www.confused.com

When talking about insurance, it's hard to ignore packaged bank accounts! These delightful products can give you huge savings on insurance (as long as you would be getting it anyway). At the time of writing the best example is the Nationwide FlexPlus. For £13 a month, you get household phone insurance, breakdown cover and household travel insurance. When I opened mine, it was cheaper for me to have this account than just breakdown cover on its own. Definitely worthwhile checking it out for yourself and working out if it would be cost effective for you!

www.nationwide.co.uk/current-accounts/flexplus

Finally (in what is a bit of a stretch to my 1-hour promise) is **re-mortgaging.** This won't be applicable to everyone, but if you have a mortgage that has stepped up to the standard variable rate, checking a few comparison sites or speaking to a mortgage broker can save you an incredible amount of money! Unless you're planning on selling in the near future, there aren't many reasons not to move onto a cheap fixed rate mortgage. A good mortgage broker shouldn't try to charge you before you take the mortgage, so it's always worthwhile talking through your options with them to see what they can do for you and how that compares to the offers you could get for yourself and what you have already. Obviously, they're not particularly impartial, as they are literally trying to sell you a mortgage, but as long as it won't cost you anything to get a quote, it's absolutely worthwhile spending the last part of your 'hour' of personal finance speaking to a mortgage broker and browsing comparison sites!

1 DAY

Introduction

The time has come to furnish our metaphorical financial palace. We're in a stronger position at present, but finances are for the future! The Bank of England aims for 2% inflation, that sounds pretty decent right? Seems like a boring statistic that doesn't mean much to you? Well unfortunately that statistic will be one of the main determinants of your long-term financial strength if you don't fight back against it! At 2% inflation, your money loses half of its spending power every 35 years! That means if you put £1000 into a bank account without interest, when a child is born, by the time they retire, it will be worth £250 in today's money! If that sounds horrifying, then strap on in! As I'm going to lay out the principles of long-term personal finance; we're going to scratch the surface of savings, home ownership, investment, and retirement. And once again, now more important than ever as we're going to be talking about really significant, long-term topics here: This isn't financial advice, you should always do your own research as well and most importantly tailor everything to your own personal situation – with that in mind, lets crack on!

Emergency Fund

There is much disagreement throughout the realm of personal finance, however one area where most people agree is on emergency funds. This is a vital place to start when we start to think about savings and investments as they're not always 'liquid', meaning you can't access them instantly when you need them and they could also go down in value, especially in the short term. A savings account may need time for withdrawal or incur fees if you want to withdraw too soon, houses can't be sold overnight, and investments may go down in value when you need them. That means that keeping aside 6-12 months' worth of money in an account that you can access straight away can be really valuable. You never know when you may need more money at short notice whether from losing your job, your car breaking down or an email informing you that you have a once in a lifetime opportunity to invest in a diamond mine in another continent!

You should decide how long you want your emergency fund to last based on your own appetite for risk, how stable your own position is in terms of your income, expenses and who you have around you to support you if things go south. When it comes to calculating how much you need, there are loads and loads of budget creators online or if you want, just use a piece of paper. You can do it in one of two ways: 1) how much it would cost you each month to live as you are now (this may be easier because you can just look at previous bank statements to see how much you spend). 2) What it the minimum you need to survive i.e. food, rent/mortgage, bills, childcare etc. I personally use the first option, you have the flexibility of moving from the normal spending option to the 'essentials' option if the time comes, but it's a lot harder to switch in the other direction. I also think that personally, if I was in a position where I needed to use my emergency fund, times are probably quite bad and I certainly wouldn't want to have to sit down and work out how I was going to cut unnecessary expenditure out of my daily living.

I keep my emergency fund in the current account that I pay my bills out of (hop back to the 'current account' section on page 10 if you want to remind yourself of my current accounts). The payments going out of that account are stable, so with a standing order going in there to cover the bills, the balance stays exactly the same every month and because it's a current account, it's naturally easy to access. Some of the other options if you want a small amount of interest include easy-access savings, the interest paying current accounts that we mentioned earlier or an easy access cash ISA.

To summarise an emergency fund has three main characteristics:

- Risk free – value won't go down
- Instantly accessible
- Duration based on personal circumstances (typically around 6-12 months)

Savings, Debt and Retirement

I've included debt with savings here because I think they can be seen as two sides of the same coin. You can think of paying off debt as 'earning' the interest rate you're paying. So, if you've got a car loan at 3% but your lowest savings rate is 1%, you would save money in the long term by paying off the car loan with the money in that savings account. On the flip side, if you managed to get a mortgage at 1.5%, and your lowest interest investment was making 2%, you would be losing out if you paid off the mortgage quicker.

Keep in mind that paying off debt guarantees that interest rate, so if you've got a speculative 5% return investment and a debt that you're paying 3% on, it's worth considering taking the guaranteed 3% by paying off the loan faster. As a wise one once said: three birds in the hand are worth five in the bush…

Savings accounts come in many shapes and sizes, and importantly it doesn't need to be labelled for you to use it as a savings account. You've got more obvious options like cash ISAs and savings accounts, but you can also use current accounts, premium bonds, Islamic banks, regular saving accounts linked to your current account, Lifetime ISAs and pensions. The four main things I consider here are:

- Interest rate
- Are gains taxable?
- When can I withdraw?
- Unique benefits

I agree, that last one is a bit of an 'anything else' cop out, but you'll have to forgive me. In terms of interest rate, the best rates shift around a lot, I use Money Saving Expert (as always) to compare them. There's not much of a point in me saying which interest rate is best at the moment because by the time you read this it will likely have changed! In tandem with this, the options based on the stock market e.g. pensions (or some ISAs) will also have variable rates of return that we'll speak about later.

The majority of people won't pay tax on their interest (unless it's from a pension). Thanks to the personal savings allowance, lower rate taxpayers won't need to pay tax until they're earning over £1000 in interest a year (£500 for higher rate). If you are fortunate enough to find yourself above this threshold, or in the highest rate tax bracket, then you can look towards lifetime/cash ISAs or premium bonds to ensure that all of your gains are tax free. It's also important to note here that because pensions are paid into 'pre-tax' you will pay tax on the interest (along with whatever has been paid in) when you come around to withdrawing your pension.

I'll use that as a door to discuss Lifetime ISAs. I won't go into vast detail as the decision to choose between paying into a Lifetime ISA and paying into pension can be quite complicated, but the benefits are potentially vast. A Lifetime ISA uses 'post-tax' money, meaning you've already paid tax on it, then you put it into the account. Now the special thing about Lifetime ISAs is that you get a 25% bonus when you pay in (up to £4000 a year), basically like the government giving you back your income tax if you're in the lower income tax bracket! Unfortunately, you can't withdraw from a Lifetime ISA until you're 60 years old (or if youre buying a house, but I'll cover that function later on). If you withdraw before this you will end up being stuck with a 25% penalty, which is basically the government taking back their bonus and 5% extra as a punishment. Because of this association with tax, I think the proper comparison to a Lifetime ISA is a pension rather than the other savings accounts.

You also need to consider employer matching or boosting when comparing the Lifetime ISA to a pension. Some employers will match or boost your pension contributions up to a certain level, which can help to massively amplify the power of saving into your pension.

To summarise, whether you'll be better off with a Lifetime ISA, or a standard pension is going to depend on five main factors:

- If you're in the higher tax bracket, it's probably better to use a pension which you pay into pre-tax
- Does your employer match or boost your contributions?
- If you're going to end up with a fat pension, you may be better off paying into a Lifetime ISA because your gains will be tax free when it comes time to withdraw
- Penalty for early withdrawal
- If you want to use it early to buy a first home

Working out which is better long term can be really challenging and is different person to person. You can rest easy knowing that both are great options and the decision between them is a matter of choosing the one that is more amazing! You also don't necessarily need to pick just one, you're allowed to have both. If you're feeling really unsure about which options are better, I'm sorry to say that I wasn't able to find a nice easy comparison calculator myself for these. However, there are lots of separate Lifetime ISA calculators and pension calculators, so you can calculate both separately and then compare. Alternatively, you can speak to a financial advisor. Of course this will cost money, but given that it's a set it and forget it type of decision that you're likely not going to have to think about for a while unless your circumstances change, the cost of a financial advisor could pay off for you.

Finally, a whistle-stop tour of some of those mysterious 'unique benefits' that I mentioned earlier. Lifetime ISAs gives you a boost of 25% when you pay in; Premium bonds pay out prizes each month instead of the same amount of interest, which can help to make saving more ***interesting***; Pensions are paid into before you pay tax and employers may boost your contributions; Islamic bank accounts pay out a share of profits instead of interest to accommodate religious laws, with the added bonus of pretty tasty returns.

Home

Onto one of my personal favourites: home ownership. You can find so many great resources online about home ownership, but you can equally find just as many landmines, with cowboys running around dishing out terrible advice all over the place. Estate agents and property investors are apparently an incredibly prolific demographic of content creators! This gives me another opportunity to drive home the message that this isn't financial advice and that you should do your own research on everything I say as well: I too could well be a cowboy! I'm not though, I promise…

If you're deciding whether to buy a home or to rent, I think the decision is a lot less clear cut than many people would make it out, it's rare that you find people on the fence of this debate, but I really do think it's a more personal decision than most people would try to make you believe! Before I dig deeper, here is a table to summarise some of the key benefits of each:

Buying	**Renting**
Home is likely to go up in value	No repair costs to the home
Interest on the mortgage likely cheaper than rent	Don't have to pay fees associated with home buying e.g. Stamp duty, solicitor fees etc.
Will eventually be owned, so costs are lower when older and property is paid off	Opportunity cost: can spend the deposit/ equity on another investment or business opportunity
Peace of mind of not having a landlord	Flexibility of being able to move often
Freedom to modify property	Doesn't exclude home ownership – can own a rental and rent somewhere else

So, should you buy or rent? Hopefully that table has given you the taste that the decision isn't as easy as many claim. As a rule of thumb, if you're going to live in a property for a short period of time, it's cheaper to rent, if you're planning on living there for a long time it's cheaper to buy. At some point in the middle, they will cost the same amount, that time is typically quoted at around 5 years, so if you were planning on staying somewhere for 4 years, you'd be better off renting, for 6 years you'd be better off buying. That time changes from place to place, there are loads of good calculators you can use online, where you can plug in theoretical purchase prices, rents, deposit amounts and mortgage interest and it will pop out the 'break even' time which you can use as a guide for what's going to be better for you on the balance of probability. Of course, you need to bake uncertainties into your decision as well! If you choose renting and you're badly wrong, worst case scenario is that you might live in poorly maintained accommodation or you missed out on an amazing deal. If you buy a property and you're badly wrong it can have a significant financial impact for years to come (this is unlikely though). A calculator only shows the financial side of the decision though! Many people say that buying a house is one of the most stressful things you'll ever do, as well as the responsibility of having to fix problems yourself and the potential stresses of renovation and repairs, the decision can't easily be broken down to a number.

www.smartmoneytools.co.uk/rent-vs-buy

I feel like I should also tackle the idea of 'your home as an asset'. When you go away to look into this in further detail yourself, you'll probably come across a small but loud group of people screaming at you to tell you that your house is a liability, not an asset. A statement which isn't completely wrong! As a principle it is useful because it draws your attention to the fact that your home will probably **cost** you money overall (check the tool above to find out how much it will cost/make you). Some lucky people will buy homes that go up in value faster than repair bills and mortgage interest payments come in, but for many, their home will lead to them losing money overall, especially in the shorter term. **However,** and this is a big however, the alternative is either renting, living with friends/family or homelessness. Home ownership doesn't exist in a vacuum! You have to consider the alternatives, and in the long term, the chances are home ownership will save you money. So it may be a liability in the strictest definition of the word, but I'd caution you to take that statement with a pinch of salt! With my rant out of the way, we can transmute this into a reflection of an earlier section of this book. With the idea in mind that your house can cost you money, rather than being an 'investment', you should factor this into your decision of whether to pay off your mortgage early. If you've got a low interest rate on your mortgage, there is often a good chance you can get better returns in other places for example savings/ current accounts, stocks/shares and investment properties. And your decision on the speed you're going to pay off your mortgage doesn't need to be set in stone, if you get a 5-year fix at 1.5%, then in 5 years' time you re-mortgage at 3%, you may want to start paying it off faster when the interest rate goes up.

Renting is seen by many as a necessity, while a mortgage can be cheaper than rent for a lot of people (even after repair costs have been factored in) many aren't able to build a sufficient **deposit** to get to the stage at which they can think about purchasing a property to live in. This is a problem that is bigger than this book can solve, however there are things that anyone can consider doing, making it a bit easier. In my opinion, the most significant option is the Lifetime ISA. This account which I spoke about earlier as a retirement style account, also has a second purpose: it can be used towards a deposit for your first home! You might remember that it gives you a 25% bonus on up to £4000 a year, this can be a great boost to your deposit, as long as the money you put in won't be needed for anything else, because you'll get penalised for withdrawing if you aren't buying a property. This means that if you can pay in the maximum amount, you can get £1000 a year essentially for free from the government to help you get on the property ladder. Other options to consider if you're struggling to afford a deposit:

- Help to buy scheme (5% deposits on new builds)
- Buying with someone else
- Shared equity i.e. Owning a portion of a property and paying rent on the percentage you don't own
- All of the financial tips and tricks we have discussed already

Given that we only have one hypothetical day to do everything in this section, I think these are outside of the scope of what we can speak about. Hopefully you can use these topics as a springboard to develop more ideas from your own research.

When it comes to buying a property, it is vital to know the market you're trying to buy in, and that's a lot easier than it may seem! I think that having a strong understanding of the market you want to buy in is a lot more about how many months you've had your eye on the market than how many hours you can sink into it in a short period of time! Using online property sites like Rightmove or Zoopla, you can save searches and get updates when new properties hit the market in the area you're looking in! That means If you decide on price, location and what type of home you want, you can spend a few hours going through all of the properties currently available and get a decent idea of what you can get in that price range and area. Then you just have to spend a small amount of time every week checking the properties that have come up this week or any price drops. If you start doing this early, by the time you've built a deposit, you should have a great idea of what a good price, bad price and the right price are for properties hitting the market. It will let you know when you're getting a deal but most importantly, you'll develop your 'Spidey Senses' so when you see a property that's way cheaper than it should be, you will know to go through with a fine-tooth comb and find out if it's too good to be true!

But that's not it, I've got two bonus tips for you here! First of all there is a Rightmove google chrome add-on which I absolutely love! It shows you the price history for every property on Rightmove, which has such amazing value when you're trying to negotiate. It will tell you how long the property has been on sale (and therefore if they may be more open to a cheeky but reasonable offer) and any price changes they've gone through while they've been on the market. My second juicy bonus tip is to use a Rightmove price range that is slightly larger than your actual range, every so often you'll find a bargain that hits your wants for a bit less than your minimum; at the top of your range you may be able to convince the sellers to come down into your range, and it gives you an idea of the difference that extra £10-20 000 makes in terms of square footage and quality.

www.propertylog.net

To round off our financial preparation for home ownership lets talk about **mortgages!** The two main routes here are going to different banks and getting individual quotes or speaking to a mortgage broker. There are some comparison sites that you can use, but I've found that they aren't amazing because they're limited in how specific they can be to your situation. The big takeaway here is that you should really consider speaking to a mortgage broker! They can be your best friend throughout the process of buying a property and in the majority of situations, their fee will be more than covered by the savings they'll get you on the mortgage. A good mortgage broker shouldn't charge you for a decision in principle. This means they will give you a 'quote' based on all of your information which you can take to estate agents and use to put offers down, a bit like proof of what you can afford (as long as everything goes right with credit checks and everything else). What that means is that you can use the broker to get a decision in principle for free, then go and get individual quotes from banks to see what they can offer you. In my experience, I couldn't get anywhere near to the mortgage brokers offer with individual bank quotes; but you may be different so it's always worthwhile checking.

Investing

What a journey! We've made it to the much-anticipated final section: **Investing**. Inflation is constantly eating away at our money, making our money worth less and less every day. Inflation becomes more and more of a problem, the longer you have money saved for, compounding in the same way that interest does, leading to huge long term impacts on your savings. When you're living pay-check to pay-check, that money doesn't have a lot of time to lose its value, so as long as your wages are going up in line with inflation (which to be fair a lot of the time they won't), you don't need to be particularly worried about the price of things going up. However, thanks to our lifechanging, mind blowing, journey through finance, with a bit of luck you're well on your way to having a fat stash of cash! So it only makes sense that right at the start of our journey, we properly arm ourselves with the knowledge we need to let our money grow with us! I also have to preface that this is an enormous topic, with many huge books dedicated to it, I will not cover the intricacies of the stock market here, my aim is very much to give you a strong introduction and guide you to further, more detailed sources.

So what are **stocks and shares?** In their simplest form, they are a way of purchasing a small percentage of a company. If a company had 100 shares in total, and you bought 1 share, you would own 1% of that company. In real life, companies have far more than 100 shares, for example owning one share of Apple would mean you owned 0.000000006% of the company. Some companies pay out a dividend to their shareholders. This is where they pay out a portion of their profits back to the shareholders based on the number of shares you have. Coca-Cola for example typically have a dividend yield of around 3%, this means that for every £100 of Coca Cola stock you have, you will receive a payment of £3 each year. This is especially impressive as the dividend per share of Coca-Cola has gone up each year since 1990, so you can be quite confident of the return. On the other hand, some companies that are more focussed on growth don't pay out a dividend and instead reinvest all of their profits back into the company in the hope that in the future they will make even more profit. With these companies, your gains are based on how much the price of the stock goes up, rather than how much the company are paying out directly.

But **what determines the price of a stock?** At the most fundamental level, the price is determined by the amount that people want to buy or sell it. As a rule of thumb, if more is being sold than is being bought, the price will go down, if more is being bought than is being sold, the price will go up. There are lots of factors which are associated with the price of the stock such as the Price to Earnings ratio and expected future profits (see further reading below for more information) but all of these factors eventually feed back into the people buying the stocks; High earnings compared to the price of the stock don't directly increase the price of a share, but they will make a hedge fund or bank more likely to want to buy the stock, which will in turn increase the stock price. Because the underlying fundamentals of a stock don't have a direct link to the stock price, this creates a lot of 'noise' in the stock price. This is why when you look at the graph of a stock, it never follows a straight line, it is jagged, going up and down repeatedly, because the buying and selling is based on the opinions of people. Different investors disagree over what the exact price should be, based on political events and reports from the company among many other things. However, over the long term, the noise of people's short-term opinions gets filtered out and (in theory) the underlying strength of the company shines through.

I found it really hard to learn about the stock market before I started investing myself, despite reading several books, and looking at lots of websites and YouTube videos, I had built up a number of misconceptions that I have slowly dissolved as time has gone on. A great tool to get past this is to set up a dummy account. There are loads of apps you can get to do this, including trading 212 which I will mention later. A dummy account is an account where you don't put any actual money in, buying and selling shares with imaginary funds as if it were a real account. By doing this, you can spend 6-12 months investing with no risk, giving you a playground within which you're allowed to make mistakes and learn the things that you weren't able to gain from what you had learned beforehand.

Now we've spoken a bit about what stocks and shares are, let's talk about a few of the principles of investing in them. From the get-go, everything I'll be talking about here will cover long term investing. There are some people who 'trade' stocks which means that they buy and sell shares frequently, making money from the 'noise' that I mentioned earlier. The majority of people that try to trade stocks in the short term will lose money; this is for a number of reasons, but the main one being that Wall Street and the big banks get their information quicker and in larger quantities, giving them a very distinct advantage over us mere mortals. Instead, we will be talking about investing for time periods of typically 5 years and over. This gives plenty of time for short term issues to balance themselves out. My goal when investing is to keep risk low while trying to ensure that I get consistent gains on my investments. This typically means aiming for around 5% a year, from a varied portfolio of companies and funds.

How varied your portfolio is, is referred to as **'diversification'**. This is the idea that by spreading your investments across multiple countries and sectors, you limit your risk. By making sure you have investments in different countries, one country struggling won't drag down your whole portfolio, in the same way that owning shares in lots of different sectors means that if one sector does especially poorly e.g. travel, the damage is limited. Of course, it's not that simple, by diversifying by country and sector, you also limit your success when one of those sectors does very well. As with all good things, it's about finding a balance, ensuring that you have sufficient diversification to limit risk, while putting your money more heavily in areas you understand well. For example, if you work in healthcare and understand the ins and outs of that market, you may be better off having a higher investment in the companies you believe in. Importantly, investing is also more sustainable and enjoyable if you love the companies you have invested in!

Managing diversification can be really tricky, fortunately most stockbrokers offer funds. These are bundles of stocks which are created and managed by a bank, so you can buy many stocks under the umbrella of one fund. The bank will control which company's stocks should be included in their fund and change or refresh the list when they see fit. Because of the work they put in, they will charge fees to own the fund; typically, the fees are low compared to the potential benefits of the fund, but it's important to remember that fees can compound and grow in the same way that your gains can. So, while a 2% fee may sound low, over 10-20 years it will build up to a very significant amount. To work out the long-term effect of fees that you will be charged, you can use a compound interest calculator online, and use a negative interest rate so a 2% fee would be -2% 'interest'. Two of the most well-known examples of funds are the FTSE100, a fund which contains the 100 biggest companies in the UK and the S&P500 which contains the 500 largest companies in the US. These are both Index funds, a type of fund that is controlled by an algorithm with little human input, and consequently, very low fees. Famously Warren Buffet, an incredibly well-respected investor and the owner of Berkshire Hathaway, challenged a number of fund managers to beat the S&P500 over a long period of time and none of them were able to do it. The other type of fund, the type managed by these fund managers, are called 'actively managed funds'. This means that they have a team of bankers/analysts who work to beat the market and give better returns than the relevant index fund. This means they have higher fees, but also gain the benefit that you can be more specific about what you want, whether that is a clean energy fund, a food production fund or a healthcare fund.

I want to finish off this brief introduction to stock market investing with three big takeaways that you will undoubtedly come across time and time again as you look deeper into this topic:

- Past returns don't predict future gains
- Be very cautious when investing money that you will need to use in the next 5 years
- Time in the market is better than timing the market

Time to unpack that! The first one speaks for itself, there are lots of funds and stocks that have shot up massively recently and it's really easy to buy into these stocks because of a fear of missing out, in the hope that the same will happen again. However, the past performance of a fund manager or company, doesn't guarantee that they will be able to do the same again.

Secondly, the goal of investing is obviously to strengthen your long-term financial position, however, it does come with the risk that your money will go down in value. Going back to the same principles around the emergency fund we discussed earlier, putting money in the stock market that you need in the short term is more akin to gambling than it is investing. If you think that investing in the stock market is going to cause significant stress and anxiety, I would really encourage you to weigh this heavily into your decision.

Finally, the immortal phrase: 'Time in the market is better than timing the market'. This refers to the difficulty/ near impossibility of working out the best time to buy a stock or fund; when you're staring at a graph it is very easy to think that you're about to find the bottom and that you will be able to buy it that little bit cheaper and get a slightly better price, but the evidence says that the vast majority of people can't do it. Based on this, we have the concept of 'Dollar Cost Averaging' (I apologise for the Americanism). This is the idea that if you buy a small amount on a regular basis rather than throwing in large lumps at once, you will perform better overall. It is called Dollar Cost Averaging (DCA) because when the price goes down, you will lose money on what you already hold but you will be able to buy more of a stock 'at a discount'. Then when the price has gone up, you won't be able to buy as many shares, but you will have made gains from the rest of your holding so it averages out over time. So for example, I have a stocks and shares Lifetime ISA in which I pay in £4000 a year, and split it between the FTSE100, S&P500 and MSCI China. Even though I know how much I am going to pay in throughout the year, instead of throwing it all in at once at the start of the tax year, I split the £5000 (£4000 + £1000 Lifetime ISA bonus) evenly across 12 months and buy each of the index funds on a regular, repeating monthly order.

Now I know that you're itching to know more about the stock market, but I'm afraid that's an itch I am unable to scratch within the confines of this book! So here are a few of my top picks for further information which I'll unpack in the final chapter, but I really wanted to mention them before I talk about opening an account:

- The Intelligent Investor by Benjamin Graham – **Stock market investing**
- Rich Dad Poor Dad by Robert Kiyosaki – **Investing and general life advice**

- Think and Grow Rich – Napoleon Hill – **General life advice with a sprinkle of investing**
- Graham Stephan (particularly index fund and dollar cost averaging videos) – Youtube - **Investing**
- Mark Tilbury – Youtube – **Investing and financial advice**
- Money Saving Expert (Again) – **Mecca of British Personal Finance**
- Alpesh Patel – **Investing advice**

Finally, now you've got some sure footing when it comes to the principles of investing, **where** do you do it? First of all, it's time to mention the ISA again. To ensure that you don't have to pay tax on those all-important gains, you may want to consider opening a stocks and shares ISA. This can be a vanilla stocks and shares ISA or it can be a stocks and shares Lifetime ISA with all of the characteristics that we spoke about earlier. All of the providers mentioned below offer a stocks and shares ISA, but keep in mind that a stocks and shares ISA will share the £20 000 limit with the cash and Lifetime ISAs, so if you've already got one of those, make sure that the total paid into the three is less than £20 000 each year. Now getting into the provider, if you're looking for a large traditional stockbroker, Hargreaves Lansdown, AJ Bell and Vanguard are three of the biggest out there. Vanguard is an American stockbroker most well known for their incredibly popular low fee index funds, whereas Hargreaves Lansdown and AJ Bell are British stockbrokers. If you're interested in one of these big companies, it is important to pay attention to ongoing fees. Whilst they will also vary on transaction fees, it is the ongoing fees which will compound and could amount to many thousands of pounds over the course of your lifetime. Always think about plugging the numbers into a compound interest calculator to get an idea of what they may cost you over 10, 20 or even 50 years. Other than my Lifetime ISA, which I use as a retirement account, I hold all of my other shares and index funds with Trading 212. They are a newer stockbroker which offer an app-based stock brokerage which charges either no fees or very low fees depending on what you're buying. They, like the others, are FSCS protected which means your funds are fully insured up to £85000. The biggest downside I experienced was that they are less supportive than the other brokers, Hargreaves Lansdown for example have beautiful information sheets which are incredibly informative and interesting, with informative insights. Despite this, I thought this trade-off was worth it. If you want a bit of a selection when it comes to cheap app-based stockbrokers, Freetrade is another great example. Once again they are free, as you may have guessed from their name, however they do have a subscription fee for their ISA. I have only mentioned a few of my favourites here, there are of course lots of other options which you should have a look for to work out what's best for you! I'll include a link to the Moneysaving Expert comparison page for stockbrokers below.

www.magic.freetrade.io/join/richard/138864b0

Affiliate Link

www.trading212.com

www.vanguardinvestor.co.uk

www.hl.co.uk

www.youinvest.co.uk

www.moneysavingexpert.com/savings/stocks-shares-isas/MSE Link

WHERE TO GO NEXT?

Introduction

Now we've finished our brief history of the financial universe, we need to add some meat to the bones. Hopefully I've given you enough of an idea for you to 'know what you don't know', now it's time to become an expert. I've split the next steps into three main categories for you to pick and choose between depending on your preferred information modality. First, we've got books, which I think are the best in terms of depth of content, but I appreciate they're not everyone's thing; so in lieu of books next are two of my favourite financial youtubers. Here you can get the wisdom of financial literature and experience condensed into video format, the downside of this is that they may leave out some useful and interesting information that you could have found in the books, and they may also have sponsorships or biases giving you an incomplete view of the financial landscape. But by the nature of videos, it is a much more digestible way to access the information. Finally, we have money saving expert, which is a great reference material, which I use almost like an encyclopaedia of personal finance. The other website-based resource I enjoy is Alpesh Patel's website and associated resources. He is a hedge fund manager who has diligently created loads of great resources around investing including a free online internship which comes with loads of great articles and e-books which are perfect to get you on the path to a strong understanding of the stock market.

Books

We're going to kick off the selection of books with the most thorough explanation of investing that I've come across: The Intelligent Investor by Benjamin Graham. This is a book both mighty in content and size which digs into the fundamental building blocks of investing. It was written over 70 years ago, but the messages and lessons still stand the test of time! It can get quite wordy at times, so I recommend making a couple of notes as you're going through, if only to make a note of the things that interested you or that you think you'd benefit from further reading on. I initially tried to go through this one as an audiobook and I ended up having to go back and repeat a lot. It's definitely one to take slow and properly absorb. I've mentioned it first because I think it will make the most substantial impact on your knowledge and understanding, but it may not be the best to start on if you're not a fan of diving in at the deep end.

In complete contrast, Rich Dad Poor Dad by Robert Kiyosaki is the perfect book to start on. It will really light a fire under you to want to start investing and start on the path of financial freedom, as well as giving you the principles of long-term wealth, the mindset of wealth and the greater system of societal views and politics around finances. It's an easy read (or listen if you like audiobooks) with a bunch of anecdotes and really interesting viewpoints!

The final recommended book is Think and Grow Rich by Napoleon Hill. If there was a spectrum with financial knowledge on one side and mindset on the other, this one is on the mindset side, The Intelligent Investor is on the other and Rich Dad Poor Dad is sat happily in the middle. I really like this book; it was written in 1937 and it has matured like a fine wine. From my experience of the personal finance space online, this is one of the most heavily recommended books I've come across and I can tell why. Napoleon Hill interviewed an incredibly large number of highly successful individuals to gain a strong understanding of which characteristics and traits led to success. His lessons are applicable to many different strands of life, however I, and many others believe his messages apply especially well to the world of personal finance.

YouTube

I have two recommendations when it comes to personal finance education, there are loads more but I've not come across many which I think have the right breadth, covering many aspects of personal finance, whilst maintaining a strong level of research and depth to their videos. My first pick is Graham Stephan, he's an American personal finance youtuber, so what he says is slightly less applicable with regard to retirement accounts, brokerages and credit cards for example. But his videos are always incredibly well researched, and he has a small number of really important and strong principles which he weaves throughout his videos. He has made a few great videos particularly on dollar cost averaging and index funds where he goes into the data and research on it, whilst condensing the videos into a short time.

www.youtube.com/grahamstephan

If you want more information that is more relevant to the UK, I suggest Mark Tilbury. He has a really great way of starting from zero on a topic, whilst still managing to make sure everyone comes away learning something new. As well as investing, Mark spends a lot of time talking about making more money and 'side hustles' which is a really valuable area of personal finance that I've not touched in this book. So, if you want more money to compound with investing, you may want to focus more on Mark Tilbury.

www.youtube.com/marktilbury

Websites

You may not be surprised by the first website I recommend, the ultimate reference material, the grand throne of Martin Lewis, the Mecca of Personal Finance: Money Saving Expert. A delightful, easy to use website which has information on almost any personal finance topic. They can help you to reduce your spending; increase your earnings through cashback, bank switch incentives and side hustle ideas; increase your saving; and improve how much you get out of those savings!

www.moneysavingexpert.com

Alpesh Patel's website is probably the biggest resource I've mentioned here and also where I will finish off the 'further reading' section because of this. Alpesh Patel is the head of a hedge fund and has spoken on national TV with regard to finance and the economy. He is dedicated to reduce wealth inequality and in view of this has created a great set of resources including a free open-entry internship which finds a great balance between hand-holding if you need it and higher level resources for those that already have a strong background understanding.

www.trading-champions.com

FINAL WORD

I hope you have enjoyed this brief guide to personal finance. I hope that you can now see that getting control of your money isn't an impossible task. You're in a position right now to set in motion practices that will put you in a strong position for years to come.

So many of the things you can do, will take 15 minutes to start, but will carry on until you retire (hopefully now at an earlier age than at the beginning of the book). Your finances don't need to consume your life to get them right! That is, unless you're an incredibly boring person like me, in which case, you should absolutely read about personal finance recreationally, then write a book about it.

I will end this book in a fitting way, with a QR code! This time, to my website, where you will find links to further content from me around personal finance, in different formats such as audio and video.

www.richardchater.com

Generic Links

www.joinhoney.com

www.topcashback.co.uk

freetrade.io

www.ingramcontent.com/pod-product-compliance
Ingram Content Group UK Ltd.
Pitfield, Milton Keynes, MK11 3LW, UK
UKHW020421250726
13967UKWH00007B/2762